Little Lucy's Family

First published 2006 by
Veritas Publications
7/8 Lower Abbey Street
Dublin 1, Ireland
Email publications@veritas.ie
Website www.veritas.ie

10 9 8 7 6 5 4 3 2 1

ISBN 1 85390 997 1

A catalogue record for this book is available from the British Library.

Extract from **Star Light, Star Bright** by Alfred Bester courtesy of Nelson Doubleday (p. 15).

Designed by Paula Ryan
Printed in the Republic of Ireland by Betaprint, Dublin

Veritas books are printed on paper made from the wood pulp of managed forests. For
every tree felled, at least one tree is planted, thereby renewing natural resources.

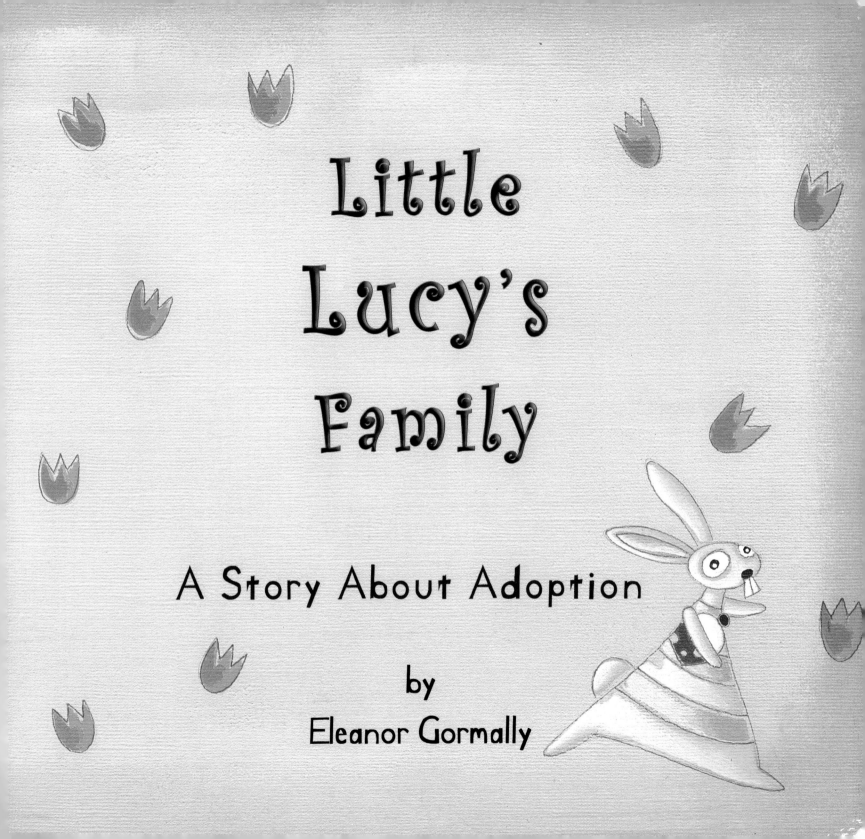

Little Lucy's Family

A Story About Adoption

by

Eleanor Gormally

In memory of Grace.

To Jarlath, Patrick and Liwa with love.

My Dad says: There are lots and lots of different kinds of families in the world.

My Mum says: There are lots and lots of different ways to make a family.

I say: My family is really special!

My name is Lucina – Lucy for short.
This is me with my Mum and Dad.
Oh, I nearly forgot Nibbles – our crazy rabbit!

This is a photograph of me with Dad and Mum and Nibbles.
It was taken last summer on our holidays.
I do all sorts of things with my family.

I love my family.
I think my family is cool!

Sometimes I think about what Mum and Dad say about families. That gets me thinking about my family and how it all happened.

First there was just Dad and Mum.

Oh, I nearly forgot Nibbles! First there was just Dad and Mum and Nibbles. Then I came ... or they came to me!

My Mum smiles when she tells the story about how she and Dad had to go all the way to Russia to take me home.

It was very cold. They wrapped me in a big, furry blanket. Nibbles likes to hide under it. She thinks it's hers!

Dad and Mum adopted me when I was a baby – just eight months old – a little hair, no teeth and a big gummy smile! Mum and Dad wanted a family all of their own. They felt sad because they couldn't have babies like other Dads and Mums.

They wondered how they might make a family for themselves. So they talked to all sorts of people about what they could do.

One night, they were watching TV. They saw pictures of a children's home in Russia. Some of the children there needed families to love and care for them.

The pictures they saw made them feel sad. Even Nibbles felt sad.

7

Dad and Mum looked at each other. 'That's it!' they shouted. 'We have lots and lots of love and kisses and hugs to share.' So they asked some important people in Russia if they knew any little child who could help make their family. And guess what? I was chosen! I think it's cool that I was the one who got to live with Mum and Dad (and Nibbles) forever and ever. It makes me special!

Most of the kids I know have a Dad and a Mum and that's that! I have my Mum and Dad. But as well as my Dad and Mum I have a birth Mum and a birth Dad. Most kids have enough to do to handle one Mum and Dad – not to mention two! I don't know much about my birth Dad and Mum; I was too small to remember them when I was in Russia.

I grew inside my birth Mum's body. She gave birth to
me – that's why she's called my 'birth' mother.
I don't know my birth Mum and birth Dad's names.
I wish I did. I feel sad when I think about it. So
I have thought up my very own name for them.
I call them my Babouskas – you know, like the
Russian dolls! I think that's a great name,
because the dolls are all inside one another
and I came from inside my birth Mum.

My Mum and Dad tell me that sometimes birth Mums are not able to keep their baby. Sometimes they are too young; sometimes they don't have enough money; sometimes they don't have family or friends around to help them out; sometimes their country says they can only have one child; sometimes they are very sick and don't have enough energy to mind a little baby; sometimes they might have died.

I sometimes wonder what my birth Mum and birth Dad thought when they saw me for the first time. I wonder what I was like! My friends have these little photos of the day they were born. I wish I knew what I looked like when I was born. I feel sad because my birth Mum and birth Dad didn't keep me. I wonder did they love me. Sometimes I get angry and all confused and don't know what to think. Sometimes I feel kind of lonely like a bit of me is missing.

One night as I was just going to sleep I began thinking about my birth Mum. I wondered where she is; what she is like; what her voice sounds like; do I look like her; does she have brown curls like me; do I have her eyes; would she know me if she saw me; does she ever think of me.

My Mum came into my room. She saw I was crying. She asked me what was wrong. I couldn't talk. I was afraid that she might be sad that I was thinking of my Babouskas. I was afraid she might think I didn't love her. So I told her I was fine.

Later my Dad came in. He loves the stars at night. For as long as I can remember Dad and I look out the window on clear nights. We see which one of us can spot the brightest stars in the sky. Then together we make a wish.

'Star light, Star bright. First star I see tonight.

I wish I may I wish I might have the wish I wish tonight.'

That night was crispy clear. So we played our 'star gazing' game.

16

Then I told him; 'I wish I knew what my birth Mum was like.' My heart thumped as I stared into his face to see what would happen. He looked at me with his big grey eyes and hairy eyebrows. He put his arms around me and held me all close.

'Sometimes life is really, really hard,' he said. 'Things can happen and nobody really knows why. But what I do know is your Mum – Oh, I nearly forgot Nibbles – your Mum and Nibbles and I, we love you to bits!

'You know, it's OK to think about your birth Mum,' he said. 'She was the one who carried you inside her for nine months and that's a long time for a tiny little baby.'

17

Then he smiled. 'You mightn't remember your birth Mum, but I can tell you a bit about her when I look at you.'

'Close your eyes …' 'Oh no,' I said to myself. 'Now Dad has really lost it!' '… think of your smile, think of the easy way you are with people, think of your lovely brown curls, think of your jokes and how you make others laugh, think of your love of snow and frost and swimming and music, think of your sense of fun … now somewhere and everywhere in the middle of all that is your birth Mum.' Then he stopped, gave me a big hug and said, 'And remember that your birth Dad is in there somewhere too.'

Saying goodnight he said, 'Your Mum and I, you know, we think about them too. Without them there would be no you and where would we all be then?' I thought of my Babouskas. Then I fell asleep!

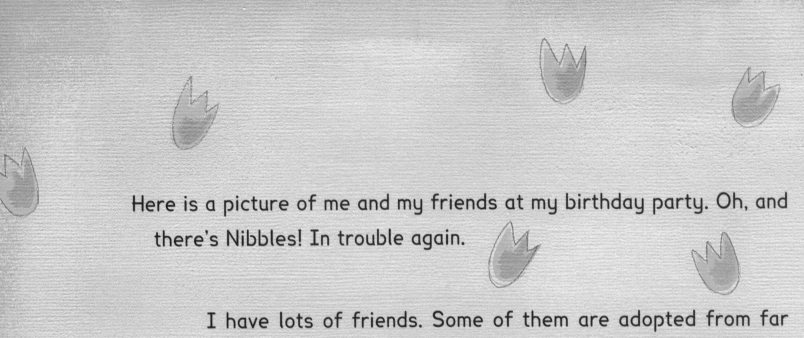

Here is a picture of me and my friends at my birthday party. Oh, and there's Nibbles! In trouble again.

I have lots of friends. Some of them are adopted from far away countries – just like me – but not all from Russia.

Vera's Dad and Mum adopted her from Romania. Jin and Mei's parents went all the way to China to bring them home! Jin and me are great friends!

Once I told Jin that I wished I had straight black hair like her. She told me she hates it when grown-up people tell her that they love her hair. They usually pat her on the head, she said. I'd hate that.

She said that sometimes people say that her Mum couldn't be her **real** Mum because she is fair with blue eyes and Jin is dark and has deep brown eyes. This used to make her really angry but it doesn't anymore. She said she knows that people who think like that don't really understand big stuff. I like Jin a lot.

One day she showed me her My Very Own Story Book. This is a really cool book all about herself. Her Mum and Dad made it for her. It tells about her life in China; the people who looked after her in the children's home; how her parents adopted her; how they came to bring her home to live with them forever and ever. She doesn't show her book to too many people. I felt very special that she showed it to me!

Jin has gone back to China on a visit. She went with her Mum and Dad when they were bringing her little sister Mei home. She saw the place she used to live in when she was a baby. She even met some of the people who looked after her! That must have been great!

Dad and Mum say that
they will take me back
to Russia when I get a
bit bigger. I think
I'd like that!

25

The other day at school we were chatting about stories. Teacher asked us to think of our favourite story. She said that we all have lots of favourites, but that usually there is one we probably like to hear over and over again.

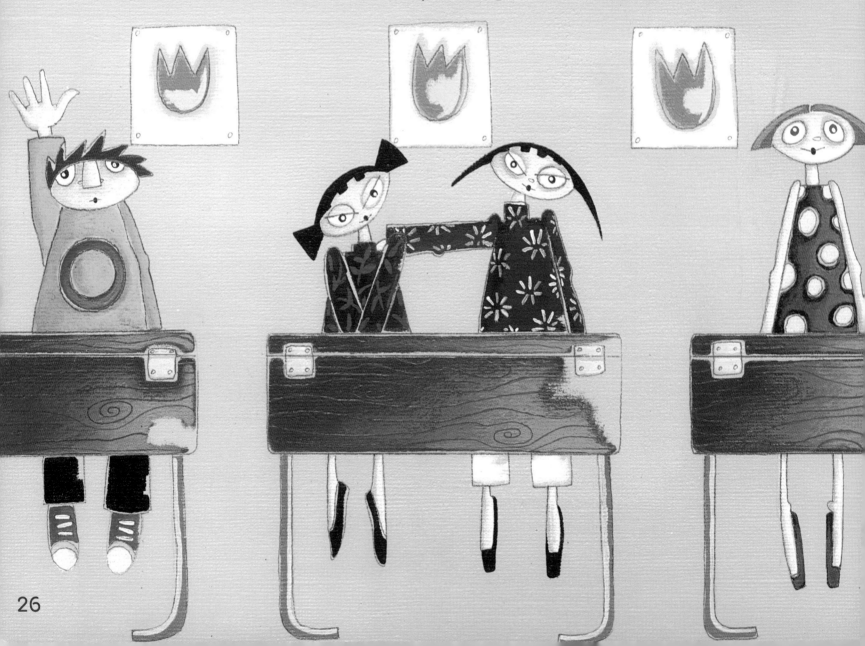

I didn't have to think too hard about my favourite story – that is, my favourite not-found-in-a-book story. It is the story of how my Dad and Mum adopted me. I love it when my Mum sits me close beside her and we look at the big green photo album that has a picture of me on the front.

I love to hear how they were all excited when they found out that they could adopt me; how they packed their bags to come and see me and nearly forgot their passports;

how Nibbles hid under their bed and wouldn't come out for them; how they cried with delight when they saw me; how I was a little strange with them at first;

how they played with me for a few days; how they were sad when they had to go home again and wait before they could come back and take me home;

how they had rings under their eyes for weeks because they were not sleeping too well – the waiting was so hard; how their hearts thumped as they took me in their arms to take me home;

how loads of people came to see me at the airport; how proud they were of their little daughter;

30

how we all slept in one big bed on my first night in my new home; how we were all learning to become a very special family. Then she stops ... but the story doesn't end ...

I get to tell my bit! This bit gets longer and longer and longer every time we tell it! That's the way the best stories go.

I love my family and I know that my Mum and Dad love me too – Oh, I nearly forgot Nibbles! I know that my Mum and Dad and Nibbles love me too.

I think that my Dad is right: there **are** lots and lots of different kinds of families in the world.

I think that my Mum is right too: there **are** lots and lots of different ways to make a family. But most of all I know that I am right:

My family is **really, really** special!